Lessons On Flying

Life's Flight Plan

For Children 8 to 80

by Majo

Illustrated by Adrienne Brown

On a cold, bright, blustery day in March, I stood at my kitchen window and watched as a female robin began to build her nest. She collected her building materials: old grass, sticks, broken branches, paper, mud…and even some white yarn. She would no sooner begin her construction, then the strong winds would start to blow. Down would tumble her hard work. I laughed and thought to myself, "Give up little bird. You might want to wait for a calmer day."

She didn't listen to me. She just kept flying back and forth, without giving a second thought to the windy conditions. Smiling, I walked away from the window and forgot about the nest.

2

A week later, I looked out and to my amazement, there it was...a perfectly constructed, round, and very compact, little home. Only days earlier there had been grass, twigs, and mud scattered all over the ground. "Wow!" I thought, "That robin did a fantastic job in spite of all the obstacles the windy weather had thrown at her."

In a few days, I noticed four, beautiful, baby-blue eggs nestled in this tiny nest. At night, the female robin would return and sit on the eggs to keep them warm and safe from nature's elements. The male robin would often come by to check on her. He wanted to make sure things were okay on the home front. I was fascinated by their dedication and support for one another during the impending birth of their offspring.

A few weeks passed before the eggs hatched. And then, out popped four, ugly, scrawny, little birds.

To me, they looked like worms with very big heads.

Oh boy, were they hungry! All day long Mom and Dad Robin would feed them. Talk about a tag team…these two were the best. The little ones' mouths were always open, constantly awaiting their next meal. When they weren't eating, they were chirping impatiently…reminding Mom and Dad that they were there. Obviously, they were not too happy having to wait for their next mouthful.

I watched all of this in utter amazement. I saw how quickly their scrawny bodies were transformed with feathers soft and fluffy. I'd check in on them every day to watch their progress.

One day, I noticed that a particular bird kept spreading its wings, so much so that it crowded out the other birds. They had to cling to each other, fearful that they would fall from their nest.

Obstinately, this cocky one, with its overzealous nature, did push one of the birds out of the nest. The little bird floundered on the cold, hard, ground below…attempting to hop along but constantly falling.

The parents went crazy. Flying overhead, they chirped their concern. It was obvious to them, and to me, that the little guy was not ready to fly. Its wings were not quite strong enough. The parental instruction was incomplete.

The Mom and Dad Robins were beside themselves as to what to do. They tried to protect the little bird by continuing to feed it. Frantic bird conversation took place. I hoped the "pushed from its nest bird" survived… although I guess I'll never know. I've learned, over the years, that, "Life is a Mystery". Sometimes bad things do happen to good people. Who can explain? It's just a mystery.

That "ready to fly bird", who caused all this commotion, took off and flew the nest. Perhaps, it had places to go and birds to see. "Look out world! Here I come!" seemed to be its destiny.

Days passed… I watched as the third little bird climbed timidly out of the nest. It carefully and cautiously edged onto the tree limb.

I thought, "Oh my, looks like it's about time to take off."

Mom and Dad Robin flew overhead, constantly encouraging the timid bird towards the sky. Flying back and forth, they seemed to be demonstrating the art of flying. "This is how you do it. Come on! Just stretch your wings… You can do it!"

For a very long time, it stood there listening to its parents' plea. The little body was shaking uncontrollably. I could see its heart beating through fuzzy little feathers. Oops, it pooped itself! Even wet itself! And then, like a flash, that hesitant little bird took off…furiously flapping its wings.

The fourth little bird sat in the nest and sat in the nest and sat in the nest. Once, I saw it step gingerly out onto the tree branch, but then quickly scurry back into the safety of its surroundings.

Mom and Dad Robin kept encouraging and motivating the little bird to follow them.

I swear I saw it shake its head… "Nope… Not Gonna do it… No way."… At least, that was my interpretation.

Mom and Dad eventually stopped their daily feedings, but they never abandoned their little one. They would fly by, merrily chirping their encouragement and showing how it was done. But…that stubborn little bird continued to sit in the comfort and safety of its nest.

As I look out my window today, I see that the little bird must have taken flight. Now there is an empty nest in my tree. However, I don't feel sad or miss them very much. For you see, I've learned many Life Lessons from my little feathered friends.

I call them *"Lessons on Flying."*

Lesson #1…Goal Setting

Set a goal and keep at it. In the beginning of our story, the Robins' goal was to build a nest. It didn't matter that the weather conditions weren't the best. The robin knew what it was born to do and kept at it until the nest was completed. Long ago I heard the saying, "Obstacles are there to instruct, not obstruct." How Empowering!! Think about that the next time you're faced with adversity.

Write your goals down on paper. Look at them often. Visualize them in your head and enjoy the feelings the visualization brings. If, for some reason, you don't achieve that particular goal…change direction. It may lead you to an even better destination.

Lesson #2…Life Isn't Fair

Some people do get pushed from their nest too soon. They don't think they are ready to fly. Maybe life has been hard on them. They've lost a loved one… lost a job… lost an opportunity… lots of reasons. I could go on and on, but honestly, life is what YOU make it. No complaining. No blaming. Definitely do not be a victim. A friend once reminded me, "In order for things to change, you have got to change." In my own life my beliefs, my attitudes, my behaviors needed to change. I am responsible. I am accountable. That became my goal. I discovered I had choices and, indeed, I was the master of my life. Yes, life may not be fair, but how we choose to live our lives is up to each and every one of us.

Lesson #3… Never Compare Yourself to Others

Some people, like some birds, were born to fly. It seems as though they always had a "watch out world, here I come" attitude. Good for them. Do you realize how much precious time we waste wishing we were someone else… comparing ourselves to others…even feeling jealous of others' success? You may feel inferior being around them. But remember…you have but one life to live. YOURS! You don't have to be THE best; you have to be YOUR best. Work with what YOU have. You'll be a lot happier and hopefully more successful.

Lesson#4… Take a Risk…It's Part of Life

The third little bird stood there for a long time. It was very frightened and perhaps thought, "I'm not sure I can do this…It looks impossible."   I was reminded of the saying, "People with courage don't lack fear."   We're all afraid of something. Failure is probably one of our biggest fears. Do you know how many very successful people failed before they succeeded?

Thomas Edison was told he was stupid. They claimed Oprah Winfrey unfit for television. Before Walt Disney was fired, his boss described him as not having imagination or good ideas.   Abraham Lincoln, Bill Gates, Henry Ford... the list goes on and on.   The moral is…take a risk. What do you have to lose? You could become one of the great ones. You might even fly like an Eagle!

Lesson #5… Let Go and Move On

The nest is empty now. I didn't see the last bird take off, but it did teach me a valuable lesson. Let Go and Move On. Don't remain uncomfortable in your comfort zone. Insanity, they say, is doing the same thing over and over but expecting a different result. Some people, like the scared little bird, sit in their nest and sit in their nest and sit in their nest. They keep waiting for life to come to them, waiting for things to change, waiting for people to change… not realizing that in order for things to change, they have to change. The hardest person you will ever change is…YOU.

Try venturing out into this big, beautiful world called Life… Let go of the past… It's over. Forgive people… after all, we're human and make lots of mistakes. Take some chances… Remember our little birds…they all faced different challenges, as do we.

Don't be afraid to spread your wings. Take a leap off that branch. Keep in mind, there is no reward without some risk. Learn how to soar on your own.

Surrender to Life's Flight Plan.

Trust me… the view will be ABSOLUTLEY AWESOME!!!

Illustrator

Adrienne Brown was born and raised in Kansas. "So early on in my childhood I was amazed by sketching and doodling". I absolutely loved picture books. As I grew up I collected all I could. I longed to be a children's book illustrator." Most of her career was in graphic design and illustration. "You name it, I have probably drawn it."

She now resides in the Mountains of Idaho with her husband and daughter. Snuggled in the mountains and illustrating as much as possible. "I love the personal collaboration with Majo and creating her characters. Helping her wonderful stories come to life is an incredible feeling. I am truly blessed to be a part of it all."

Contact Adrienne at adbrown14@gmail.com or papermoonco.com

Author Biography

Majo is a wife, mother, grandmother, writer and entrepreneur who promotes positive thinking, and achieving a high quality of life. While raising her family, she began her career as a corporate consultant, training employees in team building, sales and diversity. She also earned a real estate license, wrote a column called "The Family Hour" for a Philadelphia area newspaper and modeled in print and television. She founded three businesses to foster personal accountability, successful parenting and improving the prevalent cultural mindset regarding women in advertising.

Of all her many accomplishments, Majo is most proud of being the Mother of her eight children and grandmother of her many. Majo is a beautiful, energetic and determined entrepreneur. She has written six books for children 8 to 80. The first four, *HUMBLE PIE, THE COOL CHAMELEON, CLEO THE COLD FISH AND LESSONS ON FLYING,* are now available. *THE DRAB CATTERPILLAR, AND A DOG AND CAT RELATIONSHIP,* will be obtainable in the near future. It has taken her 30 years and many, many rejection letters to achieve this goal. The saying "It's never too late" and Bob Dylan's quote "He who is not busy being born, is busy dying" motivate Majo to keep growing.

Majo is married and lives in Smithville, NJ.

Contact Majo at her website:
MajoTheAuthor.com or email: mjbgd@aol.com

Made in the USA
Columbia, SC
01 November 2017